HELLGRAMMITE

HELLGRAMMITE

MATHEW V. SPANO

PUBLISHED BY
BLAST PRESS
324B MATAWAN AV.
CLIFFWOOD, N.J. 07721
GREGGLORY.COM

ACKNOWLEDGMENTS

"Hellgrammite" first appeared in *The Yellow Chair Review*, Pop Culture Issue, December 2015.

"What Tried To Get In" first appeared in *Quantum Fairy Tales*, Issue 14, winter 2016.

"Fly Away" first appeared in *Psychological Perspectives*, vol. 47, no. 2, 2004.

"Scarecrow" first appeared in *Middlesex: A Literary Journal*, vol. 1, no. 8, 2015; republished in *Psychological Perspectives*, vol. 59, no. 1, 2016.

"Sleeper Shark" first appeared in *This Broken Shore*, vol. 8, summer, 2015.

"Wading the Rio Grande" first appeared in *This Broken Shore*, vol. 5, summer, 2012.

"Grouper" first appeared in *This Broken Shore*, vol. 9, summer, 2016.

"Merlin" first appeared in *This Broken Shore*, vol. 9, summer, 2016.

"Empty stringers" first appeared in *Identity Theory*, Spring 2006 Poetry Selections Issue, March, 2006.

"An angry sky" first appeared in *The Piedmont Literary Review*, vol. 19, no. 4. 1996.

"Communion Cup" first appeared in *The Heron's Nest*, vol. 14, no. 3, 2012.

"Blueberry Picking" first appeared in *The Heron's Nest*, vol. 14, no. 4, 2012.

"Seventh Inning Stretch" first appeared in *The Heron's Nest*, vol. 12, no. 4, 2010.

"The Bootprints End" first appeared in *The Heron's Nest*, vol. 11, no. 2, 2009.

"Town Cannon" first appeared in *The Heron's Nest*, vol. 11, no. 3, 2009.

"Extra Innings" first appeared in *Modern Haiku*, vol. 36, no. 2, 2005.

"Spring Cleaning" "Extra Innings" first appeared in *Modern Haiku*, vol. 38, no. 2, 2007.

"Mockingbird's harsh cry" first appeared in *Modern Haiku*, vol. 31, no. 3, 2000.

"Back to school" first appeared in *Modern Haiku*, vol. 30, no. 1, 1999.

"Imagining old age" first appeared in *Modern Haiku*, vol. 39, no. 1, 2008.

"Winter river—an old-timer's fingers" first appeared in *Modern Haiku*, vol. 32, no. 2, 2001.

"Valentines Dusk" first appeared in *Simply Haiku*, vol. 6, no. 2, 2008.

"Roadside Leaves" first appeared in *Simply Haiku*, vol. 6, no. 2, 2008.

"Fall" first appeared in *Simply Haiku*, vol. 6, no. 2, 2008.

"Rainy Day" first appeared in *Simply Haiku*, vol. 6, no. 2, 2008.

"Summer Funeral" first appeared in *Simply Haiku*, vol. 6, no. 2, 2008.

"Pop Up" first appeared in *Simply Haiku*, vol. 6, no. 1, 2008.

"Funhouse Music" first appeared in *Simply Haiku*, vol. 5, no. 3, 2007.

"By dawn" first appeared in *Frogpond*, vol. 26, no. 3, 2003.

"Tropical fish tank" first appeared in *Frogpond*, vol. 12, no. 2, 1999.

"Winter river—voices" first appeared in *Frogpond*, vol.25, no. 2, 2002.

"Winter wading" first appeared in *Frogpond*, vol.29, no. 3, 2006.

"Vacant Resorts" first appeared in *Frogpond*, vol.28, no. 3, 2005.

"Desert Find" first appeared in *Middlesex: A Literary Journal*, vol. 1, no. 8, 2015.

"Tardigrade" first appeared in *Middlesex: A Literary Journal*, vol. 1, no. 8, 2015.

"Tonkin Cane" first appeared in *Middlesex: A Literary Journal*, vol. 1, no. 1, 2008.

"Ghost of a Heron" first appeared in *Middlesex: A Literary Journal*, vol. 1, no. 1, 2008.

"When the Light No Longer Lingers" first appeared in *Middlesex: A Literary Journal*, vol. 1, no. 6, 2013.

"The Acorn Sowers" first appeared in *Middlesex: A Literary Journal*, vol. 1, no. 6, 2013.

"Comic Book Artist" first appeared in *Middlesex: A Literary Journal*, vol. 1, no. 7, 2014.

"Geppetto Finds His Boy" first appeared in *Middlesex: A Literary Journal*, vol. 1, no. 6, 2013.

"Death Comes An Angler" first appeared in *Middlesex: A Literary Journal*, vol. 1, no. 7, 2014.

"Matching the Hatch" first appeared in *Middlesex: A Literary Journal*, vol. 1, no. 4, 2011.

"Ephemeroptera" first appeared in *Middlesex: A Literary Journal*, vol. 1, no. 6, 2013.

"Surface Lure" first appeared in *Middlesex: A Literary Journal*, vol. 1, no. 6, 2013.

"Mantis Shrimp" first appeared in *Middlesex: A Literary Journal*, vol. 1, no. 8, 2015.

"Midstream" first appeared in *Middlesex: A Literary Journal*, vol. 1, no. 7, 2014.

"Enlightenment" first appeared in *Middlesex: A Literary Journal*, vol. 1, no. 7, 2014.

"Salamander" first appeared in *Middlesex: A Literary Journal*, vol. 1, no. 8, 2015.

"Bacchus and Apollo" first appeared in *Middlesex: A Literary Journal*, vol. 1, no. 4, 2011.

"A Crossing" first appeared in *Middlesex: A Literary Journal*, vol. 1, no. 7, 2014.

"Catch and Release." first appeared in *Middlesex: A Literary Journal*, vol. 1, no. 6, 2013.

"*Rivers and the inhabitants of the watery element are made for wise men to contemplate, and for fools to pass by without consideration.*"
—Isaak Walton, The Compleat Angler

"*There was a long tug. Nick struck and the rod came alive and dangerous, bent double, the line tightening, coming out of water, tightening, all in a heavy, dangerous, steady pull. Nick felt the moment when the leader would break if the strain increased and let the line go. The reel ratcheted into a mechanical shriek as the line went out in a rush…*"
—Ernest Hemingway, "Big Two-Hearted River"

"*I sat there and forgot and forgot, until what remained was the river that went by and I who watched… Eventually the watcher joined the river, and there was only one of us. I believe it was the river.*"
—Norman Maclean, A River Runs Through It

I

WADING THE RIO GRANDE

Choose your boots carefully—
felt soles with cleats for clinging
to mossy stone down deep runs.
Seek out a durable staff—you'll need it.
Carve it yourself
from mahogany, oak, or hickory.
Bone it,
treat it,
and find in its handle the head of a wolf, eagle, or colt.
Always cut with the grain.

Wet your lines so they flow into supple knots —
surgeon's, cinch, slipknot—
Tie them slowly,
ease into the stream,
and remember the current's quiet force,
unrelenting.
Wade upstream and you're spent in three strides.
Better to move with the current,
careful never to cross your steps.

No one walks on water here.

The young priest, who preached catch and release—
a fly fisher of men, he would free tangled rainbows
from an abandoned stringer, nailed to a tree on the far
    bank.
He could feel the current between his thighs
but could think only of crossing over.
They found him crucified in the deadfall.

So it is best to arch your stride—
dangle one leg downstream and rock
like a bow-legged cowboy.
Midstream, you'll find the saddle-shaped boulder:
with your toes, feel for footholds—stirrups.
Here you can straddle the river,
and ride up high on a shimmering blue mare—
but mount quickly
or she may change course
and crush you like a cornered rodeo clown.
Here, the current cleaves, the cattle drive splits
and crashes around you on all sides.
Here, you can cast lines like lassos
in every direction.
Or let the current do it for you.
Let line slip through the guides
and tangles loosen by themselves.

WHEN THE LIGHT
NO LONGER LINGERS

Where does the light behind the eyes go
when it leaves the body
no longer a body but an object in a room—
a coat rack, an end table, a chair piled high with clothes,
a rag doll with eyes gone cold and black?
Something vital leaves them dull,
never to come back,
a thing less animate than the machines
that whir and whistle on
even when the light no longer lingers.

A child, I hooked a rainbow
and brought it to the bank where it gasped and flailed
until the gills slowly ceased to flap,
the eye finally went dim and flat,
though I tried to make it swim again
in the backwater darkening pink.
I envisioned the light lift from its eye
and flow where it danced downstream,
in the dappled sunlight
that rides glistening rapids
above the flat black rocks.

A man, I hooked a body once
and pulled it onto the dock—
a duck hunter on a pram overrun
by spring rains and rapid runoff—
his body a log long submerged,

his clothing tattered trash bags,
hollow sockets where eyes had winked and wept,
black holes that could drag down
even the brightest stars...
Still, I searched for the soul's quick glint
stowed away to survive the full fathom five,
and found it in his pocket sealed in cellophane—
a message in a bottle, firefly in a jar:
a single photo of his son,
stringer raised high, with rainbows all aglow—
his eyes kindled by a new sun
rising without and within.

ROOT OF THE MATTER

A swift Sligo gale exposed her art—
uprooted Beech caught in the act,
the unbleached bones shown in her womb.
Some Gaelic youth, his tomb undisturbed
since before the Normans,
now dangles, tangled in roots,
strangled by slow serpents,
skull sucking earth matter,
soil-filled sockets,
reborn in bark, leaf, bud—
umbilical Uroboros.

Mother of the Woods, you lie revealed:
Beech Queen who suckles the starving
with tree nuts, hard nipples, shelters
with wide branching embrace--
Queen Bitch, who can sap a young soul,
rewrite him, a character
in her endless (de)composition,
a single page in her ancient book,
Beech leaf.

THE ACORN SOWERS

Gather a thousand tree nuts
into an old burlap sack.
Stow it in the back seat,
to sow them where you may,
and set a course for sunrise.
Roll down the window and hurl
a fistful to the wind wrapping round windows
as you hurtle, Johnny Appleseed,
down dawn's highway.
Some will fall on rocky soil, some on thorns
or scorched earth,
but some will root deep to burst blacktop,
push past property lines, uproot posts,
arch across a neighbor's fence,
crack through concrete.

What will spring from what you've sown?
Hickory, spruce, chestnut, oak—
some reach deep into city streets,
broom-handle bats for stickball.
Some seed the brain's strange branching—
textbook, yardstick, pencil—
unfurling in scroll and diploma.
Some sing in a Stradivarius,
soar in a model glider,
crack rawhide in a Louisville Slugger.
Some dance on unfamiliar waves
or darken the sky in feathered volleys.

Tree of knowledge, tree of life,
budding into awareness.

COMIC BOOK ARTIST

The page, a calm sea—
moonlight masking
teeth and tentacles,
stalked eyes scanning surface
for the slightest (disturbance).
My pencil, casting lines in loosening loops—
a spell to summon serpents.
With short strokes, I brush the surface
to tease demons
from the dark beneath the page.

Something ascends
to slowly nose the lure,
a shadow lingers there,
deeper than my darkest shade.
A violent thrash
bursts the surface, the pencil straining,
playing something big,
feeding taut line
to an unplumbed hunger.

Fingers cramping, I slowly draw
forth an eye enraged, bottomless maw,
stiletto studded,
followed by flailing feelers
and writhing coils,
finishing with a forked tail
tipped with venom.

But as I envision him hanging,
my glorious catch, glass-eyed over the mantle,
with a last lunge held in reserve,
he rips free and races for the open sea,
plunging deep into the vanishing point.

GEPPETTO FINDS HIS BOY

On Opening Day, my son and I squat
on the rocks of the trout stream, spinning
yarns of leviathans asleep in deep runs
that undercut willow roots clinging
to the far bank. He wonders if he'll hook a whale
with teeth like cutting spades,
and a maw like a yawning cave.

Who's to say he's wrong?
That sperm whales only hail from seas
five hundred miles east,
feeding on squid at six thousand feet,
not the flies we drift along
a six-inch, sweet-water creek?
To a boy, such replies sound shallow,
desiccated by statistics.

Who's to say some Monstro doesn't prowl these pools
waiting to wolf down a whaleboat
with a hide that sheds harpoons
and frayed cables from which dangle
bloated corpses of sea captains, and sucker scars
from an epic tangle with the Kraken—
lone leviathan left behind from a time
when all was prehistoric sea, mythical beast
bursting the surface from a fifty-fathom dream
pushing inland to invade the controlled flow
of this state-stocked stream?

I'm ready to be swallowed whole
as I set out in search of my son,
and he ready to rescue me,
even if we end up squatting on the steps
that lead down the monster's gullet,
catching tuna scraps from its last meal,
telling tales round a flickering fire,
our mast the last of our kindling,
waiting to be swallowed,
to be reborn to each other.

GHOST OF A HERON

I

This time too, I look for him
just beyond the next river bend,
behind an outcropping of granite
through the strands
of the weeping willow
the old fly fisherman wrapped
in morning mists,
hunched,
the ghost of a heron,
just another birch branch
tangled in deadfall.

Until his arm begins to sway,

keeping time to the river's pulse.
the fly rod suddenly spews serpents,
sidewinders,
hissing like Moses' staff,
sideways figure eight,
settling on the current,
parting the waters.

II

Blue-Winged Olive—
he makes it flutter and flit
to his spell
along the reeds' edge.

Spent, it lies suspended
as he freezes rapids
out of time:

Before the fish strike,
before the rodent's quick shriek—
not even the shrike.

A small splash,
a precise sip,
and the fly-rod arcs,
his tense line tapping
the current that courses through
muddy creek and Milky Way.

All the river's pulse and passion
in the air dance of
this one wild trout.
Granted its meteoric runs,
its black hole gravity,
its orbit slowly tightens
as it ascends
into the ragged net
of waiting fingers.

Among empty stringers
he pulls the ancient rainbow
out of the fog—
an old hook-jaw,
colors faded,
accented by a few bolt-shaped scars:
lightning piercing rainbow.

III

A new incantation now—
he can hypnotize a rainbow,
turn it upside down,
rock it to sleep—massage with water
the pulsing gills
and pluck the small fly
from the abyss
beyond teeth and tongue.

Stepping back
into the clear current,
he feels the old hook-jaw gather
into itself the ceaseless flow
of days and seasons.

And it vanishes.

The current drives ahead
into another Opening Day.
and in his favorite spot
a boy with the same rhythm
casts for eternity.

ORACLE

The old timer tried to slather my eyes
with mud and spit to wash away blindness.
Where I would watch the same old stretch
of rocks and rapids, he could discern
the speckled trout suspended,
tucked in the current's slim seam,
just behind the tractor tire with the worn treads.
Where I would stare stupidly
at the weedy shallows,
he would spot squalls of swirling tadpoles,
snail tracks mapping the muddy bottom,
a crayfish vanishing like a magician behind
a puff of silty smoke.
Where I would see only the water striders
twitching across their usual routes,
he would witness mayfly nymphs,
tiny dragons clinging
to bottom crags, then sublimating
into angels ascending on solar sails
in spiral clouds up shafts
of dappled sunlight.

"Dig with your eyes," he advised,
but I had only a blunt spade.
"Don't try too hard: just place yourself in the path
of visions—turn on the floodlights, turn off
the spotlight." But my spotlight wouldn't stop
and frantically scanned for any signs
of spectacular prison breaks…
and missed them always.

"See the space between surface and stream bed—
suspension of shiners and grass shrimp lacing
the long hair of the river; that turtle scaling
the half sunken log, mini submarine surfacing,
tiny tank crawling to warm itself, claim its station
among eight siblings all lined up
like stepping stones to the sun."

Then one day, without intention or special effort, I saw—
all that he did and more. Bandages unwound,
the veil lifted, cataracts cleared—whatever I imagined
materialized from the murk revealing itself
in a ceaseless stream of epiphanies—
and I a naive wise man bearing paltry gifts
to the virgin birth.
But as Passion follows epiphany,
vision becomes a curse, the old seer yearns
for the womb's dark warmth
but must bear the cold burden of his gift:

I saw frog feet still twitching
from the strait lips of water snakes;
mink like dark demons dragging rainbows
down into networks of caverns carved by river roots
clinging like claws to craggy banks;
the shadow of an osprey sending fish flashing
right into range of the heron waiting frozen,
bill gleaming like an ice pick poised;
baby pike staring aimless, gap-toothed,
belly big with her too-slow siblings;

gleaming wedding band slid
from an angler's finger or hurled there
when he chose to abandon career and family
and follow the river toward oblivion;
the slumbering corpse of the newborn
set adrift by a distraught teen—Moses sans his basket;
a submerged issue of *Time*, 9/11 still kicking up
clouds of debris from the silty bottom.

Death Comes, an Angler

Death comes, an Angler,
luring us with hope
like rising mayflies,
driving his hooks deep,
sapping our desire
to plunge back
into the vital current.
No hiding among the rocks
or the deep tree limbs.
Death draws us writhing,
out of our world,
mouths agape,
wide-eyed and gasping.

Until we are raised, finally
released
from our heavy element,
of murk and shadow,
into sweet breezes and birdsong
threading through blossoms,
limitless light spilling
from the never-ending sky.

II

MATCHING THE HATCH

We begin beneath heavy river rock,
dark and wet, we are stream nymphs, naiads,
tiny dragons in disguise—
all mandibles and claws clasping
our stone for dear life, fierce yet terrified,
until we dare to spread our swimmerets to catch
the bubbling riffles of childhood.

Headlong, we hurtle into the deep run of adolescence,
bursting the surface film, emergers unfurling
waxen wings. Clumsy and crumpled,
they fill slowly with the sun's soft pulse.
We are tiny dun sailboats, seeking to break the surface
     tension
and ride the wind
or be engulfed by some leviathan trout.

Downstream, adulthood:
we are angels ascending, spinners circling shafts of
     sunlight,
finding our green place to rest a while
among tangled tree limbs. We mate on the wing
then fall back to the water to drop our eggs,
depth charges lodging deep in the riverbed.

Where the current slows, old age: spinners spent
we spread flat our slack limbs and ragged wings
back upon the waters,
giving ourselves back to the ceaseless current—
ephemerae.

EPHEMEROPTERA

Mayflies, we would rise from the rapids,
burst the surface tension,
and unfurl dun wings to the honeysuckle breeze,
tiny sailboats taken flight
up dawn's shafts that pierce the mire.

Our time served underneath river rock,
clinging for shelter against the ceaseless current,
eluding the long fingernails of the deep freeze
and the silver strike of rapacious trout,
groping through murk and flood,
each seeking a sweet death in the other.

Emergent, we morph into the madness
of a life distilled to a single day—
large eyes to detect the other's heat,
to drink each other's light utterly.
Mouth parts vestigial, eating only ether,
forelegs elongated to clasp one another,
spin and spiral up sun shafts,
Paolo and Francesca fulfilled,
to mate mid-air, swoon in a death dance,
and charge the eternal streaming with the seedlings
of our ecstasy.

HELLGRAMMITE

Bite the jaws
that bite at you.
Let them find you lodged
in the throat
of the choked beast,
mandibles locked
even in death.
Pierce the toes of selfish giants,
return their blood
to the ceaseless current.
Heed midnight thunder
igniting your lust
from the murk
under river rock
where you like to drag
straggling damsels and knights.
Crawl the ancient path once more,
out of the depths,
onto the rocks,
spanning the moat
over ancestors' bones...
to your own dark corner,
where you can shed yourself
sans cocoon,
sprout dragon wings,
fangs,
haunt lonely streetlights
on the waterfront
spoiling for a fight over a girl—
tiny Brando, fleeting Dean,
Kill-devil,
demon seed.

HELL HATH NO FURY

Who conjured the Bobbit worm
from no cozy hobbit hole but a black cauldron
of ancient rage boiling up beneath the Aegean?
Was it Medea and Lorena, Ariadne and Dido—
    wrathful coven
who buried the spring-like coils in the sea bed,
armed antennae to wait for a wandering Puffer,
a pumped up Jason or Theseus,
bloated Aeneas or John Wayne on the prowl?
He cruises in, swollen, looking to pry open
some naïve little clam—
no Hillary Clinton or Clytaemnestra—
spread her wide to his pricks and poison.
Creeping closer, he trips the wire,
spike trap triggered—rapid fire surprise:
the invisible worm that flies in the night,
snake from a can that strikes
with toxic fangs to pop his charm,
pierce his ego, paralyze his will—
the rapist raped,
castration via the witches' worm,
the bait that bites back.
It sucks him into the sea bed
to be devoured
like Don Juan dragged to Hell.

HAGFISH

Double, double, turbulence, trouble—
pluck the plane into flame and bubbles,
plunge the cruise into our spiraling brew,
sprinkle debris on our carrion stew.

We, the sea hags reason can't reach,
the sisters only folklore can teach.
From the ocean of sleep, the sea of your tears,
we spawn and swim in your teeming fears.

Vampire kiss, tongue studded with teeth,
writhing eel body in a slime coated sheath.
The serpentine demons the heavens cast out
into the pit of superstition and doubt.

Off the map's edge where sea monsters lurk,
fathomless, silent, hidden in murk,
beyond all reckoning, all stars to steer by
the slippery knots that none can untie.

Rise from the depths of the Devil's Triangle,
await the dead fruits the dark lord dangles:
schooners, whalers and battleships sunk,
bombers, copters, the prop crashed by the drunk.

Worm into mud, lie there concealed
as sharks cruise in to make off with the meal;
Then cast a spell, a thick cloud of slime
to clog up their gills and smother their crime.

Drill deep into Moby Dick's skull,
stream through holes in the Titanic's hull.
Corkscrew every passenger's eyes,
leech the dark between the stewardess' thighs.

Dine first class on the businessman's brain,
twisty straws sip from vacationers' veins.
Like lobbyists, stuff the senator's mouth,
devour him from the inside out.

Suck last regrets from the captain's brave heart,
slither through all of his logbooks and charts.
Find the black box with its diminishing pings,
but tell not a soul of the drowned beast with wings.

Double, double, turbulence, trouble—
from the bloated dead breast we suckle,
gaze into our dark abyss,
dare to fathom our deep soul kiss.

SURFACE LURE

What will it tease to the surface?
What summon up from the dark?

Some silver-finned hope
From a jewel-speckled school?
Or a bottom feeding fear
with an Angler's ancient fangs?
A joy that breeches
and suckles young in shallow seas?
Or a spiny pride
easy to take offense, bristling with quills?
Writhing regrets,
breeding eels' slimy coils?
Or iridescent dreams that school and dart
streaming toward the sun?
A sluggish blue-grey grudge,
a sodden log to snap a line?
Medusan jealousies
with tangled tentacles that sting?
Or deep desires
with venom-tipped tails?
A phosphorescent faith
flickering
up from eternal night?

Choose the surface lure wisely
for the depths come alive with eyes.
And though they spawn leviathans,
yet it holds some power to conjure.

SLEEPER SHARK

A kayak bobs, driftwood,
strip of old bark twitching
atop the maw of the North Atlantic.
Thirty minutes for the weighted line to bottom out,
the hook baited with bloated herring
mixed with blood from twisted fingers
and sweat dripping from a knotted blond beard.

Then, the steady tug of a Greenland Sleeper
eyes feeding parasites, feeding glow worms
that lure the herring too close to the jagged dark.
Icy giant, somewhere beneath
the living and the dead
stalking down deep
stealing seals as they sleep,
reindeer and moose, antlers and all,
even polar bears stunned in the silent twilight
by a nightmare that bursts through ice
ancient invader of our waking life.

The line frayed, the rod moaning low
under the strain of the leviathan load
lumbering two thousand feet down,
dragging
the small craft like so much seaweed.
A steady, grueling retrieve, the sun sinking,
sinews snapping, no reprieve in the ancient struggle
to see if night might be hauled up
toward the sun...or if light can be capsized,

drawn down and drowned
by the heavy
depths.

Out of the murk, up from the pit,
the leviathan lolls, strength sapped at last,
as gaff, hooks and cords lash it fast,
a thousand pounds of dark matter,
amassed over centuries, now neatly cleaved
into steaks, cured of their poison,
to become the darkness in the angler's glare,
the menace in his low drunken laugh,
the silence that outlasts his tale.

MANTIS SHRIMP

Stowaway
tucked among the Pacific colony
of tiny sponges and mollusks,
well behaved citizens
of the hunk of living reef
sneaked through customs
for our saltwater tank in the Suburbs—
the greater tank within which we had swum
half asleep all our lives—day-to-day,
nose-to-glass, end-to-end.
But this lethal larva, assassin seed,
alien breed, embeds deep
in coral crevices, a sleeper cell
that slowly grows, surveilling
with stalked eyes, periscoping
from a black crevasse, until,
spring loaded claws cocked,
it is ready at last to mug a passing angel,
gobie, damsel or dragonet—
pet store clowns swimming their rounds,
blind to the wild beyond the glass
or that waiting beneath the filter.
Blackjack blow from the deepest shadows—
dirty work of a baby-faced gangster
who always plays the innocent pawn,
poor prawn ready for the plate, the perfect cover.
Nature's oxymoron: tiger shark shrunk
into a shrimp shell.

After our fish went missing,
the crabs, one-armed knights, came hobbling home,
flesh streamers from armor split,
white flags trailing the death march.
Then the ornaments were vandalized,
treasure chests smashed, divers decapitated,
the shipwreck with fresh holes punched in the hull.
We called in the experts—
triggers and scorpions
straight from *Pet Palace*,
but the next morning...only bubbles
rising from the filter, winking as they burst
the poker-faced surface.

When we tried to dislodge the little Dillinger,
he tasted our tactics with anxious antennae,
hunkered deeper, eyes pivoting
in all directions, peering infrared,
reading our souls,
marking our hands with the scars
that earned him the alias "thumb-splitter."
Finally cornered,
this swashbuckler,
with a single shot from his flintlock fist,
blasted a hole
in the aquarium glass
and rode the torrent to freedom,
sweeping us up in his black pirate wake.

That night, we served him as sashimi
and, to honor him properly,
took vows to taste and share even more
his passion for shattering glass
to return to the sea.

III

SCARECROW

He hangs, a husk
on a wooden cross
beneath the rusted windmill and empty silo
on a hill outside of town—
the only cornfield left, a patch
ripped from a generation past,
ornament for the new pox
of pressboard mansions on electric green lots.

Children pause to mock him
as they cut through his kingdom unchecked
in their daily pilgrimage from school to screen.
They taunt him to come down from his cross
and play a while in the twilight
and tweet his image with hashtag jokes
and leave plastic bottles and spent syringes at his shrine.

Tonight he will rise
with the harvest moon, blood moon,
to slash tires with a rusted scythe,
sweeten diesel tanks with sugar
to silence bulldozer and backhoe,
snatch up logging stakes and spike sycamores,
cut phone cables and fell cell trees,
fracture foundations and torch trailers.

But all the children will see the next day
is the same boney frame draped
in tattered flannel, moldy hat atop
a burlap sack with black hole sockets

that suck their souls
and a jagged mouth, loosely stitched with old shoelaces
undone a little more than the day before
in what might be called Earth's grimace
or her gaping grin.

MIDSTREAM

No one knows how he reaches
his island among the rapids
where he baits and sets his lines,
sits on his rock,
and waits…
There will be time for his meal
of wild trout in a black pan seared
over a fire of brush and twigs,
of pine nuts and blackberries;
the canteen captures evening rain.
Time will reflect
on all the current has given
and taken away…
the family and fortune, a life overflowing
and flown away, swept clean by the flood.

Right now, he breathes…
in and out,
in the branching of blood
through temples and toes,
the strength of bone and tendon,
the humors flowing their daily rounds,
the cancer seeping into his gut,
the seed still stored never to be sown.

In the waters downstream he hears
echoes, murmurs...
bathing in their song.

No Job,
he chooses not to sit on a burning heap
of ash and dried bone
and bellow out his "WHY?"
to an indifferent F-5.
Instead, he waits....

The rock warms
in the noon sun,
rapids crashing all around.

ENLIGHTENMENT

Be one with Nature, said the guru
winking his only eye.
One with leeches and tapeworms,
legions of e.coli teeming in Bambi's gut,
the mangy Tom that snatched Snow White's birds,
and Cinderella's mice spreading the Plague
once the princess ascended her antiseptic castle.

Be one with hysterical hyenas
that drag off lion cubs into the blackness
packed with eyes, numerous as the stars.
One with the F-5 that ripped through a school
stealing even the breath of a child's final whisper.

Be one with the lust that stings the straying husband's
      loins,
And the mantis that masticates her mates.
Be one with the malarial mosquito
that sighs softly in the ear of millions.
Surf the tsunami and hang ten past crowds
of the drowned that wave and gape.
Be one with the tumor nestled in the brain's pillowed
      folds,
or the one suckling like a newborn at the mother's soft
      breast.

Be one with Nature…
or with the Wise Potter at his wheel,
intelligent designer, crafty spinner

of hells on earth where the meek and mild
inherit their daily rounds, spiraling
down Dante's infernal rings,
to the nadir of enlightenment.

SALAMANDER

My rake rends a glowing grave
of maple leaves shrouding the autumn lawn,
cauldron of molten gold,
the guts of which broil up
microbial stew, smoldering
witch's brew of black fire
among the steaming heaps.
I have disturbed a demon sleep
deeper than the garter snakes
that glide just beneath
the stained glass surface.
The Lord of the black furnace
writhes forth flashing fire,
convict lexicon glaring
for all who would dare to seize
a flailing tail, swallow a flaming sword.
This one's growing new limbs,
his kin busy dissolving the belly
of a precocious pit bull,
who ate three before his heart finally seized.
Gills gone, he flees the winter breeze,
diving into flame, swimming through magma
on his long journey East
back to the fiery palace of Prester John.

MAN O' WAR

Venomous Portuguese crone,
the ghost of Mad Maria on her throne,
gypsy fortune teller who sees all
with her floating crystal ball—
she ushers the unwary into the past,
behind a curtain of beaded glass,
net of burning brands
dangling all the way to African sands.

Her crew lashed paralyzed prey:
hooks and ropes to haul and flay,
stuffed the holds with suffocation and pain,
forged misery of human chains,
stretched tentacles over time and tide,
an embrace long, deep, wide.

Her ship a bloated purple fist,
severed at the wrist,
still clutching a cat o'nine tails,
strings of bleeding entrails;
souvenir of a slaver's brain
trailing its Medussan train
still scudding the Middle Passage,
due north on its endless voyage
to bustling suburban ports,
crowded weekend beach resorts.
Arms unfurled wide
to trade winds and tide,
carrying remembrance
in a stinging semblance
to shock sunbathers awake
with locks of coiled snakes.

GROUPER

I, Goliath, I—
king of fishes,
lord of shipwrecks—
last master of the *San José*,
galleon too laden with gold,
outstripped, outgunned, lost wager
paid in blood off *Isla de Barú*.

I, Goliath, I—
hold fast
at my post, last gunner,
keep the watch
for salivating salvors
looting stores for pieces of eight.
I wait.
Spear-fishermen,
wreck reapers,
defiling the dead,
I wait
down the gunner's store
in ambush to snatch their catch:
swallow whole, inhale all,
engulf amberjack, snapper, shark—
a diver's arm reaching in for pesos,
a hand grasping in the dark
scrounging ceramics—
I splinter spears, snap line like sinew,
crack rods like backbone.

Behold my yawning maw—
blacker than the hole
a cannon ripped
through broadside hull.
My jaw built to crush crustaceans,
crumple a carapace like a mail coat.
My girth greater than half my length,
Goliath, I—
heavier than five divers,
stronger than eleven.
Even barracuda back down
when my primal boom
sounds the depths,
my twenty-four-pounder
still firing.

THE LAST LOBSTER

With a moray's madhouse gaze,
its gap-toothed grin,
ten tentacles splayed wide,
suction-tipped,
the child presses her will,
and her luck,
against the smudged glass,
testing the last lobster
who tastes her presence
and glares back in silent defiance.
He measures his last moments,
assesses his defenses,
calculates her movements,
no longer craving dark crevices.
Antennae anticipate the child's advance,
her sticky fingers inching up the glass, itching
to plunge and pluck the prize,
like the steel arcade claw she once saw
that clamped down around
a bright red bath toy.
He gauges her stalking, stalked eyes
locked, waiting,
the ragged rubber band that binds
his larger left claw frayed
to a single strained strand—
ready at any moment
to snap.

KATYDID CHORUS

A secret society
of snitching schoolgirls,
antennae twice their body size,
all abuzz on a summer eve
with the news, the burning news,
ignited from dried thighs
rubbing together,
that *she did it*—
burst a precious vase,
shattered virgin crystal,
then lied to her loving parents.
Their cliques all a-clicking, all atwitter
along their insect net.

A coven of hissing crones
perched in barren branches,
who testify *she did it*—
stole from the church basket
to feed her bastard son—
who boast they'll strike her down
with a bolt from the black,
new-moon sky.

A jury of gossips,
whispering guilt or innocence,
deliberating,
dropping rumor from the eaves
of the inn, the false claim
she did it—
poisoned the newlyweds
in a jealous fit.

A summons
for the killing frost.
Their whispers razors
endlessly scraping the strop.
Their mandibles
able to pierce even the warm flesh
of tiny mammals.

WHAT TRIED TO GET IN

After a wild night of wind and lightning,
my wife, wide-eyed in the ragged moonlight,
awakens to my hoarse whisper and anxious claim
of something large clambering across the gabled roof—
what sounds to me like the gnawing of rafters
by hooked teeth and jagged claws.
Dismissing my hunch with a sigh and a yawn,
she waves me back to bed
convinced a nightmare must have galloped
through my sleep and lingers still
insatiate, just outside the stable gate.

But whatever landed with a thud a moment ago
likely sniffs out the loose seams in the shingles
through which to pry a portal large enough
to slip through with folded wings
and retractable talons—
some wretched Grendel
dropping like a fallen gargoyle,
dead to reason, bent on stuffing our young
into his great scaly purse bulging with the bones
of neighborhood kids whose parents somehow
didn't sleep lightly enough.
A shape-shifter perhaps, slithering
through vents and shafts,
puffing dream dust into our eyes to set them spinning,
Hell bent on bolting down bone and brain
while we doze disarmed, warm near the hearth
of our own private Heorot.

My menacing knocks on the ceiling,
convey my meaning: Morse Code via Louisville Slugger,
give this bugger pause to prick up pointed ears
and listen long for me listening for him
in the leaden silence—
each of us plotting the other's next move
till, perhaps preferring easier pickings,
he surely lifts off into the gloom of the half moon
no trace by daylight of his intended invasion, save the
	gutter—
utterly bent, no doubt, by debris brought down
by the howling storm—bulky broken boughs
that are somehow now nowhere to be found.

I V

DESERT FIND

A Winchester rifle, leaning,
since 1883, against an ancient desert tree—
rusted barrel, cracked gray stock, cradled
and resting in the juniper's long embrace.
Who left it, just for a moment
frozen,
lost in the Great Basin,
shadowed from the stalking sun?
A lone prospector, his last stand,
fending off coyotes circling
a dying fire?
Defective defense for a Paiute brave
who chose to go back to the bow?
An outlaw squatting low
over the stolen gold and holey bones—
he placed it there "nice-and-slow"
as he raised his hands for the posse
in the moon's turncoat glow?
The miner's means to a well earned lunch,
jackrabbit spinning slowly on a spit,
seasoned, shaded by the old juniper?
Twilight Zone time traveler
who found the modern meds to cure his son,
then stepped back over the rim,
leaving this antique behind?
The final solution rejected
by the Civil War vet headed west,
running from nightmares,
walking away instead
into the desert dawn?

Only the juniper knows
but it whispers nothing
to the rabbit-eared researchers
who never heard of Stevens' jar from Tennessee.
They mummify it behind museum glass,
so now there's just the tree.

BACCHUS AND APOLLO

The road into Rattlesnake Gorge sloughs
along jagged cliffs. Tattered by rapids, its asphalt skin
stretched and torn by ice flows and floods,
its sloughed python skin,
its dead old snake spine
bears one more pilgrim's heavy tread.
For a half life, I have shuffled along,
seeking an opening down
to the river, a clearing to step
into the current.

Only the noon shafts wing this deep
to conjure rainbow trout
that pierce the osprey's quick eye.

The gleam from a mink's humpback—
he feels the sun's quickening dart
and stiffens, bolt upright, unsure of his escape route.
A volley rains down on the waiting mayfly nymphs
exciting them to spread wings wide and begin
their Maenad dance.

A sudden still—
then, trout flash for mayflies, tripping
the osprey's dive, scattering the mink to its dark den.
When it's over, whispers from the laurels
and sunlight on the clearing
down into the current.

COMPOST

Two heaps left steaming for years:
I have received a sacred meal,
a gift from the Great Mother,
offering her dirty dugs to dig up
in the dawn's milky mist.
Sinews straining,
I pierce the teeming stew, pitchfork probing
not only the dark decay
but also some things new
blindly writhing in the morning light:
black salamander still flailing its severed tail;
wolf spider scaling a rusted tine,
freezing on a black leaf, its own pitchfork teeth
tasting the air for fear;
slugs slipping genital-like
through earthen slits trailing lethal slime;
night crawlers lapping loam ;
black beetles scuttling beneath an unknown stone;
grubs wriggling like restless infants rooting
in her warmly corrosive cleavage.
Empty cicada shell,
infant Tithonos trapped babbling
for eternity;
deserted king of hearts—his wound now necrotic;
mylar balloon, its shriveled skin
still noosed by a pink streamer strangling
a shredded "Get Well";
apple core, coffee grounds, egg shells, grass;
candy wrapper, peach pit, rat skull, glass—

last record of lives slowly swallowed back,
duly digested by SHE who whipped up
this whole heaping mess, funeral fodder,
her heaving mounds
suckling infant corpses.

MERLIN

I inspire spitfires.
Backyard feeders my buffet.
Nothing outstrips me;
I kill on the wing: down skylarks,
devour doves,
pluck dragonflies from silver surfaces,
lock onto lunatic bats,
bogies that won't elude me.
The wizard bears my name,
my gift to raise boys to kings,
hatch empires, seize the sky for queens:
Lady hawk for Mary and Catherine.
Freya fashioned a cloak of my plumes
to give gods flight to span worlds.
Yet birders with greedy lenses
seek to shoot me down, reduce me to a digit:
I elude their count.
Even Audobon's keen eye failed to freeze
my ceaseless flight.

FISHER KING

Shattered mannequin
on a sofa propped,
you gape carp-eyed
at a flickering stream that teems
with ghost fish flickering
across a backlit screen.
Here, you can neither sit, nor stand, nor lie,
numb to the droning phone
lodged in your groin,
the rod remote dangling
from your limp grasp.
Alone, adrift,
you troll for meaning—
last drop
of blood or tears or semen
trickling down
the cheap plastic shaft.

Can you ever dig deep
into a rusty can of night crawlers,
finger a fat one,
stretch it from its hole,
palm it writhing,
pulsing
piece of fertile earth?
Plunge a hand
into an icy minnow can to trap
quivering fins, darting
and slipping through the cage
of your quickened fingers?

Feed the sharp jerk
on the charged line sinking
into the darkest hole?
Electric run of a rainbow—
steady surge that summons
the ceaseless current,
re-routed briefly
into your resurrected grasp?

TARDIGRADE

Posing on a pencil point,
cute as a comma,
tiny moss piglet
plodding, pudgy-legged, through the plot
of the Great Mother's tome,
through chapters each ending
with a great Negation:
trilobites trimmed,
T-Rex and pterodactyl,
expunged and redacted;
mammoth and sloth
blotted out in Her onslaught.

Tardi bear, ready to brave
radiation enough
to melt a man to his socks.
Hardy badger, steady
under pressure more crushing
than the sea's deepest crevasse.
Shrugging off absolute zero,
blowing bubbles at the boiling point,
Her toughest little tyke
who tucks himself in
for ten years without a bite
or a drink in the middle
of the long, long night.

Till he wakes in a drop of dew
ready for breakfast before his next big test:
more asterisk than astronaut,

naked in space all alone,
he can suck up the void,
vacuum the vacuum,
till he tumbles toward the next blue dot,
carrying Her biography,
himself the final period
in our all too brief epitaph.

CATCH AND RELEASE

I cast a fly into the darkness
where the stream runs deep like blood
and hooked a salmon big as a child
from a time before the Flood.

I took pity and cradled it close
in the backwater clear and slow
until it twitched to enter the run
and its spirit began to flow.

It looked at me with mournful eyes,
but I held it by the tail
until it turned itself into Jesus
pulled down from the rusted nails.

He turned the stream to wine-dark red,
his weight too much to bear;
I staggered to hold him in my arms
and gulped a last breath of air.

Lest I drown, I let him go
and to a salmon he returned.
Resurrected, he leaped the falls
above rapids that boiled and churned.

Another may eat of his flesh
and partake of that sacred meal.
I choose to troll my own depths:
strange fish fill my creel.

Haiku

imagining old age
in the river mist
the ghost of a heron

snow erasing
the garden's features—
teaching my dad to shave

spring rapids—
father and son untangle
their fishing lines

trout season
the current re-unites
old friends

the old angler—
it slipped through his net
the autumn moon

blood moon
drawing us together
the hush of the surf

an angry sky rides
the river's surface; from fierce
thunderheads, trout flash!

beach resort, season's end—
patio music plays
to the night surf

vacant resorts—
car sounds come and go
with the night surf

slow current—
line slips through the guides
tangles loosen themselves

first noble truth:
a hooked trout dangles
from a branch

mockingbird's harsh cry—
brook trout still swimming
against the net

on the walk back
following my own footprints
waves come and go

sandcastle ruins
horseshoe crabs return
to spawn

tropical fish tank—
fingerprint smudges
on the "Do Not Touch" sign

spring flood
mixing all the watercolors
to make mud

by dawn, the angler
has his limit—the first rays
dance on the river

shivers of dawn
scattered on the river
the loon's silhouette

trout rising—
my caddis fly lost among
ten thousand raindrops

winter river—
an old timer's fingers
slowly tying flies

winter river—
voices from the rapids near
the empty bench

winter wading—
a submerged summer issue
of *Time*

old-timer—at the end
of his fishing line dances
a green kite

empty stringers—
the old man pulls a rainbow
out of the fog

back to school, calm woods—
centerfold fades and wrinkles
on the riverbank

sleet-coated line—
the heron and I glare
at each other

opening day—
small boys tell of their catches,
their arms widening

opening day—
in the old fisherman's spot
a boy with the same laugh

communion cup
in the wine's surface tension
my uneven pulse

the dark river
pulling out a fish
with a man's eyes

Good Friday dawn—
the boy tries to release
the dying trout

the bootprints end—
the brook keeps flowing
into the deep woods

TWO STORIES

Fly Away

Two days after Christmas, I am fly fishing the rapids coming off the Razorback Gorge, a deep and sometimes dangerous run of the south branch of the Black Bear River. The trees are rust-colored, brown, black, and gray; there is no wind. Ice keeps clogging the guides on the fly rod; the only sound is a solitary crow whose call goes unanswered. I am alone on the river. Despite the neoprene waders, thermal long johns, and insulated boots and socks, the cold's talons pierce my foot bones. I submerge my fly rod in the frigid currents—ironically, the best way to clear the guides of ice—and cast again just to get my blood flowing. About twenty minutes ago, I had a bite on a size 18 pheasant tail, and it's just enough to keep me here shivering for another hour or so. To drive my thoughts from the icy sting in the toes of my right foot, I think of the Gorge in the warm seasons. The old-timers named it "Razorback" because of the odd cliff formation through which the river cut its path centuries ago: When the April sun is just coming up, the cliff casts a shadow in the shape of an enormous hump-backed boar on Jackson Valley below.

I remember one spring when two ospreys lay claim to these waters, out-fishing even the old-timers, and drawing resentful, icy glares. I tipped my cap to them, a male and female, as they juggled their magnificent catches in mid-air—brookies, browns, and bows— manipulating them to face the direction of their flight, cutting down on the wind resistance. They snatched so many trout that they surely must have had an impressive nest, packed with downy chicks, their distinctive, needle-sharp beaks constantly open to the sky. One Tuesday morning, I found both ospreys washed up on the bank, the massive, hooked talons now dangling lifelessly in the current. Although I never found the poison or the entry points of any bullets, I knew that healthy osprey don't simply drop into the river in mid-flight.

Like melting ice-flows, my thoughts drift slowly to spring times of long ago and Peter O'Shea, who learned to think like an osprey and became the best damned fly fisherman I ever saw. When we were kids, my friends and I occasionally bumbled along the banks of the Black Bear River with our oversized K-Mart rods, dangling bobbers, and coffee cans stuffed with pale, half-dead night-crawlers. And we would inevitably come upon Peter, already on his way back with a full stringer of magnificent trout that he had caught on dry fly with an ultra-light fly rod he had made himself.

"Gentlemen," Peter would address us, "if you want to catch trout, turn yourself into an osprey. Up, up and away you go! A few hundred feet up, the sun warms your back like a spotlight from heaven and you're center stage, gents! The big time! There's nothing else in the universe but you and those trout. That old spotlight reaches right down into the riverbed and shows you EXACTLY where they're hiding—those caverns 'n crags where you just KNOW the big ones love to hole up!"

By the time Peter and the rest of us reached high school, he was a local legend on the north and south branches of the Black Bear River. A straight-A student in biology, Peter dreamed of getting a Ph.D. in entomology. He had already learned much from the river—not only about the mayflies, caddis flies, stoneflies, and midges that he studied every day during fishing season, but also about the net of relationships that linked them to each other; to the various trout species; and to the pike, osprey, mink, and fly fishermen that, in turn, fed on the trout. Raised on his uncle's horse farm, Peter began practicing the 10 to 2 o'clock fly-casting motion before he could ride or even walk. I had known him since grammar school, but we were never close. Peter never got too close to anyone—he seemed happiest when he was alone fishing on the river. In high school, despite his success on the athletic field, Peter was never popular, never part of the "in" crowd— that is, those of us on the football team. He had a slight build: barely five-foot-five and sinewy, with a whippy strength that made him a star in track and field. No one could touch him in the high jump and the pole vault. Still, he was always too frail for football. Every week it seemed that Peter had a different girlfriend; he had a knack for always landing the bombshells, to the annoyance of all of us football players. Maybe it was his puckish grin and boyish humor that drew out their maternal instincts. But Peter's first love had always been the river—his first mother.

After turning over a thousand rocks in a hundred different stream beds, he became such an expert that he could predict the species and stage of the aquatic insects on which trout were feeding on any given day. On opening day, he would hold court at Razorback Gorge, spouting to anyone who would listen the Latin names for each of the mayfly species and the times we could expect them: "Now, gentlemen, let's review. There's *Ephernerella subvaria* in late April; *Ephernerella invaria* in May and June; *Ephemera guttulata* by mid-June. How can you hope to know trout if you don't know the mayfly?" Later on that opening day, some of us from the football team grew bored of watching Peter catch practically all of the trout in the river, so after a few beers each we lay on the bank, started lobbing stones into the holes he was fishing, and taunted him.

"If you could be any animal you wanted, what would it be, Phil?" I asked innocently.

"I dunno," Phil answered just as innocently, "maybe a lion or a bear. What do you think Peter would want to be?"

"You mean Tinkerbell over there?" Now, I set the hook. "Maybe a goddam mosquito—you know, a little prick?" We rolled around on the bank guffawing. Proud of my joke, I continued: "Maybe a little mayfly—ya know, they kinda remind me of Tinkerbell!" More guffawing. Peter turned to face us, but he looked more curious than angry, as if he were seriously considering my suggestion. He waded over to the bank where we looked up at him, snickering.

"A mayfly—now there's an excellent idea, gentlemen, although I'm not sure how you Neanderthals stumbled onto it. You know, you can't beat the mayfly for its sheer angelic beauty and its short, intense life. You spend most of your year-long life in the stream, eating and growing. Then you wake up one morning to discover that, overnight, you have grown long, beautiful wings. As if by magic, you're reborn out of the water and mate on the wing as you fly up toward the sun. Your winged life would last only twenty-four hours—one day of sheer euphoria."

It was the way he said it that made us all stop laughing—he ended up in a whisper, almost as if he were in a trance, as if he were living out the mayfly life cycle in his imagination right then and there. And we too fell under the spell, fantasizing about what it would be like. We suddenly felt foolish and clumsy with our thick lines laden with lead split shot. No one said a word as Peter waded off and proceeded to catch four more trout where we had just lobbed our stones.

We once saw Peter catch over seventy-five trout in less than two hours at the Gorge—an awesome feat, on the Black Bear River un-matched to this day, that aroused the jealousy of the old-timers, the old cynics. "That candy ass fly boy!" they said loud enough for everyone to hear. "Dopin' up your flies with that goddam chemical attractant? How much you pay for it over at the Pro shop? You wanna buy trout, go to Shop-Rite! They got a special!"

I was there at the gorge when Peter caught "Grendel's Mother," the fifty-pound pike that prowled the deep labyrinthine runs that wind through the gorge's network of boulders. No one knew how she entered that part of the river, but that she had taken up residence there was no fish tale. You could always tell when Grendel's Mother was near when you hit "dead runs" in the river—areas where the trout stopped biting, even in optimal conditions, even during a hatch. Those few who had tied into her had had their lines snapped early on in the contest. If the stiletto teeth didn't shred the dainty 7x tippets designed for small brookies, then the sharp black rocks around which she wrapped their lines and then bore down with all her weight and the current's force would snap off the lines even at the thickest part of the leader.

Some speculated that Grendel's Mother probably knew when the trucks from Fish and Game were coming to stock; indeed, she must have bolted down a few netfuls of brookies that spring before Peter went after her. He used a two-fly rig with wire traces, ingeniously tying on two long black Wooly Buggers, one larger than the other, with strips of tinsel in them. It created the flashing effect of a chase, the larger baitfish in hot pursuit of the smaller. As he worked the deadly dance through the water, a small river chub bore down on the rig, nibbling at the tail of the lead bugger. And then Grendel's Mother exploded from the shadows below. She swallowed both Buggers plus the astonished chub in one tremendous lunge. Realizing he couldn't simply horse her out of the water, Peter played her masterfully, letting her take out as much line as she wanted, the wire traces neutralizing her teeth and the cutting rocks, and he worked her into a shallow pool. Standing in a Charlie Chaplin-like position, his large fishing boots heel to heel, linking the rocks along both sides of the narrow feeder channel, he dammed up the pool and cut off the only exit. And then he just let her swim as fast and as hard as she wanted, around and around that pool, until she had spent all of her strength and rage. While Grendel's Mother hung suspended in a slack-jawed stupor, the needle-like teeth completely powerless, Peter simply reached in under the gill cover and lifted her clear out of the water in triumph. A small crowd of anglers had gathered, and even the old-timers grudgingly tipped their caps. They stood in awe of her nearly five feet of densely packed muscle, armored in rows of bronze scales like chain mail; her sleek torpedo outline that belied her massive girth; her enormous dragon head with its furious, blood-red eyes, and, of course, all those teeth.

I helped Peter transport Grendel's Mother, in a trash can filled with water, from the Black Bear down to the Mill River, where they had recently started a pike stocking program. I had to push my father's old pickup for all she was worth, Peter riding in the bed, wrestling with the trash can come alive, repeatedly slamming the lid back on whenever the pike's head burst through. We carefully unloaded Grendel's Mother and revived her in the backwater. She lay motionless, letting us help her until she felt the strength of the current in her blood again. With a single, gator-like thrash, she knocked us both off balance, hard onto our backsides in the river, and disappeared in a flash behind the spray and commotion.

Aside from the adventure with Grendel's Mother, I never fished much with Peter. He was always on the move, looking for a new section of the river that no one had ever heard of or where no one would ever have thought to fish. But he always fished the Razorback Gorge in the early part of the season. He was only eighteen when he died while fly fishing the gorge. It was springtime again, and the river was swollen and running fast from the runoff and recent heavy rains. No one, not even the old-timers, would dream of fly fishing when the river was so violent.

Peter waded out confidently into the shadow of the great boar. Apparently, he tried to cast too far out over the river, and his line snagged on a partially submerged sycamore branch far out in the middle of the rapids. Drawing him in, enticing him to get a better angle to retrieve his fly, the river lured and finally caught him—she tripped him up, spun him around, played him along through the rocks and into the deep run, where he drowned. Peter was reported missing, and his uncle had to wait almost a full year before the body was recovered. Big Jake Fulsom was fishing the gorge for carp with his customary bait-casting rig, twelve-pound line, and dough balls. Jake was one of my buddies from the football team, a fellow lineman, and he used to tease Peter mercilessly (whenever he could catch him) by wrapping him in an enormous bear hug and then picking him up over his head and spinning him around, despite Peter's angry protests.

On that morning, Jake snagged his line on what he thought was a submerged log, and, not one to give up his rig without a fight, he began to slowly haul it to the surface. Forty minutes later, he reached beneath the surface to grope for his hook and felt what he thought were branches and river grass. He soon discovered they were Peter's slender, pliant arms and his long blond hair. The old-timers heard Big Jake's screams from nearly a mile downriver. They reported that Jake had found Peter with the fishing line wrapped around him like a burial shroud, binding his fly rod fast to his side. They said that his body was remarkably well preserved by the cold, spring-fed run—his alabaster skin, large clear eyes, long blond hair, and even his puckish grin frozen in time.

Perhaps this was the river's way of honoring one of her young lovers, transforming him into a *puer aeternus*, her very own Adonis. I'm not sure why exactly, but it was around that time that I took up fly fishing, and I haven't fished any other way for the last twenty years. Peter would have been thirty-eight now, like me. I sometimes try to picture what he would look like. Would he be a professor of entomology, balding, with a goatee and tweed jacket, smoking a pipe? Would he have kids of his own? As hard as I try, I just can't imagine it. What would Peter ever do with a dirty diaper or a child's inner ear infection anyway? What would he do with standardized testing or a teacher strike?

My customary hour waiting for a bite runs out, and it's just as well, since all ten toes have gone totally numb. It's time for the ceremonial last cast: rod tip toward the sun, then toward the ground, over the left shoulder, over the right, and cast—the fly line tracing the sign of the cross before it shoots out over the water. As I retrieve the pheasant tail, still expecting the miracle of a strike, even a nibble, I think of the next generation of mayfly nymphs lying on the frigid river bottom. With their slow pulses, they cling to the undersides of rocks, waiting so patiently for the return of spring, waiting to emerge and fly toward the sun.

TONKIN CANE

The boy in the cellar pretended not to hear what was going on again in the kitchen. The woman's voice growing shrill and hysterical as she cursed the man, who, the boy imagined, stood on the opposite side of the kitchen behind the counter, hands in his pockets, staring blankly out the window. He would say nothing, infuriating the woman even more...and soon sounds of dinnerware breaking and doors slamming, slapping and shoving would filter down to the dim cellar. That these were his parents didn't seem to matter anymore. He didn't seem to matter anymore. They were locked in their own eternal drama, and the world around them disappeared.

In the halflight of the musty basement, he cradled the box that had been waiting on the front porch when he arrived home from school. He had smuggled the long brown package down through the angled doors of the walk-up cellar before anyone knew that he or the package had arrived. As the argument mushroomed into a full blown fight, he realized no one would look for him for hours. He had the one thing he prized most of all—time alone to dream. And now that he held the split cane fly rod kit that had taken months to arrive from China, he could set to work. The old Chinese man had promised it to him, the one who had fished with him for the last two years before vanishing. The boy never found out what had happened to him, whether he had died or gone back to China. In the weeks just before he stopped showing up at their fishing hole, the old man had told him that the kit would arrive soon—a gift to remember him by, and their timeless afternoons spent fishing together.

As he pulled the cap off the cardboard tube, an exotic smell wafted up—the smell of wood, but a strange kind of wood. The old man had said that the split cane bamboo rod blanks came from Guandong Province—Tonkin cane. The boy knew it was the best for building fly rods. He envisioned the groves where it grew, lush and green, deep in the tropical valleys of inactive volcanoes, the bamboo fed by the black soil and the long, humid summers. It was humming with life, just as the old man had described it.

Out of the long, dark tube, he poured the tiny, silver rod guides that glistened like tears in his palm. He found the spool of fine silk thread, to wind around the guide posts fastening them to the rod blank. Finally, he reached in and pulled out the cork handle. Before he set to work, he took the empty cardboard tube and held it up to his lips, making strange, bellowing animal sounds—like those of a wounded creature or an abandoned tiger cub.

As he ran his fingers up the smooth wood, he thought more about the day he had met the old man. It had been a rough day at school; the big boy with the pierced tongue had beaten him in the bathroom again. The boy imagined that in place of the bully's tongue stud there was a large silver fish hook lodged in his mouth. He would set that hook harder and deeper, again and again, as the bully flopped helplessly in the current, then reel him in, exhausted and beaten...at the boy's mercy. As he stumbled out of the bathroom, trying to conceal the blood flowing from his nose, the only one who noticed was the nice girl with the thick glasses. She offered to walk him to the nurse, but he burned with shame. It didn't help matters that he thought she was pretty. He walked with her to the nurse's office, but as soon as she left, he continued on to the school's front entrance and left.

He had gone more than a mile before he realized he was running through the woods, instinctively heading to his "safe place"—his fishing spot along the river. To his surprise, he found the old man in his spot, sitting quietly with his rod by the river. The boy studied him for a moment before approaching. He seemed to be very old, yet his dark eyes glistened merrily like the sun dancing on the river. His face was gently wrinkled, like the ripples in the slow current, and he wore a baseball cap and a faded green field coat—like something the boy had seen in old war movies. Without moving, he spoke to the boy.

"Tough day," the old man began. Was it a question? The boy didn't answer, but covered his bloody nose with his hand again. "Sure was a tough day," the old-timer repeated. "I've been sitting here all morning, fishing meal worms in this beautiful hole where I know there are fish…and I've caught absolutely nothing. Not one bite." He turned now toward the boy. "Maybe you'll have better luck?" He held the rod out, handle first. The boy hesitated, but the man seemed so old and harmless, he finally stepped forward, took the rod and sat down on the bank. After all, this was *his* fishing spot. In minutes, he had caught two fat rainbow trout. As he released the second, the boy wasn't watching the fish, its colors flashing as it diappeared into the current. Instead, he was studying the fishing rod.

"Did you make this?" he asked tentatively, his curiosity getting the better of him. "I mean, it's not graphite."

"No, it's not. And yes, I did make it." The boy took the handkerchief from the old man, nervously wiping off the blood that he had unintentionally smeared on the cork handle. "I meant for your nose." The old man gestured that he should clean up his face.

"Do you think you could teach me to make one?" the boy asked in a small voice from underneath the handkerchief. The old man smiled, and his wrinkles expanded like the ripples in a pool after a pebble has been thrown into it.

Over the next few weeks, the old man brought the pieces to build the rod in his old knapsack. For a worktable, they used the trunk of an enormous oak someone had felled with a chainsaw. As they worked, the old man told the boy that he used to make these fishing rods out of bamboo when he was a boy in China. His mother had taught him. Most of the fishing in the region was done with nets, and she had taught him the skill as an art and a pastime, as her father had taught her. Occassionally, they would sell a rod that was exceptionally beautiful. He remembered the time when he was very young and a typhoon hit. She took him up to a cave in the hills, instructing him to work on his fishing rods until she returned with his brothers and sisters. It worked. He loved more than anything to work on these rods, and the fine, intricate work distracted him from the savage winds and punishing rain. Almost an entire day had passed before he realized that she had not returned, nor did he ever see her or his brothers and sisters again.

The old man said he remembered working on his fishing rods when people called Manchus conquered somebody called the Ming (the names sounded odd and mysterious to the boy). Later, some of the groves were thinned by people using the bamboo canes to make pipes for smoking something called "opium." They faught and died over it while he sat quietly working. While "Boxers" killed even more, and the Japanese invaded and other people that he loved never returned, he polished and honed his lovely fishing rods. Again, during the Cultural Revolution, he found himself in his cellar workshop, splitting strips of bamboo, measuring, and marking. He built simple rods for bait fishing, but he hadn't started to make fly rods in this way until he came to America and learned all about fly fishing. Building split cane fly rods carried him through his new country's war with Korea, a "cold" war, the murder of a President, another war (this time with Viet Nam), the collapse of a wall, and 9/11. Now, he was beginning to feel tired, he said, and he felt it was time to pass on the art to someone new.

When they finally finished the bamboo fly rod they were working on, the old man showed the boy how to cast it. From that moment on, every day, after school, the boy raced to the spot deep in the woods along the river to practice casting, moving his forearm from 10 to 2 o'clock and back, pretending to scratch his right ear without moving his upper arm or wrist. To find the open space to cast, the old man taught him to wade out to the big, saddle-shaped rock in the middle of the river. It was summer, and they wore shorts and old shoes—the boy his old sneakers and the old man his sandals. The boy was startled at the quiet, unrelenting force of the current far out from the bank. He clung to the old man's arm as though he were grasping a strong tree limb.

The old man taught him not to move against the current, not to fight it. Wade upstream and his strength would be spent in three strides. Better to move with the current, being careful not to cross his steps. He learned to arch his stride, dangling one leg downstream and finding a foothold before transferring his weight—he felt like he was walking like a bow-legged cowboy. But it worked. And if he were ever to be pulled under by the current, the old man said, he needed to remember not to panic. Just let the river take him where it wanted to before releasing him, as they did with the trout they caught. Once, the old man remembered, he had been wading across a stream in early spring. He was wearing thick waders, which quickly filled with river water when the underwater bank he was standing on gave way. Down he plunged. Realizing quickly that he could never pull himself up with the weight of the submerged waders, he let himself fall until he hit the rocky bottom. Then, he said, he simply started to walk along a trail of rocks along the bottom. After a few strides, the trail gradually sloped back up as he approached the opposite bank. He emerged waterlogged and cold, but alive. He called that his story of the underwater bridge.

After some more wading practice, they were able to make it out to the large, saddle-shaped boulder that rose up out of the current in midstream. The boy approached it from the downstream side, letting the boulder shield him from the current and gathering his strength to hoist himself up. After helping the old man up, he looked around. Up, out of the current, he felt freer than he had ever felt in his life. Here, the current cleaved around the boulder, crashing all around them like a stampede of wild horses. Here, they cast their fly lines like lassos and pulled enormous brown and rainbow trout from behind the rocks. When the line became snagged, the old man taught him to release line and cast it out again beyond the snag before giving it a sharp yank—in this way, he could pull the snagged fly from the opposite direction, freeing it. And when the line became tangled, the boy learned to let out more line, letting it slip through the guides, pulled out by the current, so that the tangles loosened by themselves.

One morning, as they sat on the rock preparing their lines, the old man pulled a surprise out of his knapsack. "A kite?" the boy asked. The old man smiled as he unfolded a broad green kite with thin bamboo strips notched and interlocked for the ribs.

"In China," he said slowly, "this is called 'Kite Fishing.' But I think it's really the only way to *fly* fish." After a pause, he burst out laughing at his own joke. The boy frowned skeptically. Securing the fly line to the kite, he then tied a thin dropper line off the main line, down a few feet from the kite. To the dropper, he tied a large, heavy streamer. And to the streamer, he then fastened a trailer—a small dry fly, a caddis, to match the hatch that had begun to rise around their feet, but that was at its most dense downstream a quarter of a mile. It was an inaccessable spot where the river was wide and wild. Finishing his last surgeon's knot, he handed the rod to the boy. "How am I supposed to cast this?" the boy asked, still frowning. "Just get it into that gentle breeze—that's all you have to do." The boy swung the rod carefully in broad arcs, just a few times, and then the breeze caught it. He stripped line from the reel as the wind pulled the green kite downstream. When it reached the hatch, the boy stopped and let the kite hover there, the lures skimming along the current. Suddenly, the kite plummeted as if it had been shot out of the sky. Below, there was a tremendous commotion as they glimpsed a large, square black tail thrash and slap the water. It took half an hour for them to work the massive rainbow around the rocks, against the current, and up onto the rock. After releasing one hook-jawed monster, the boy began to dance on the rock as he cast his line out again, spontaneously leaping lightly from one foot to the other to the rhythm of his casting. The old man laughed and called him Sun Wukong, the Monkey King, who once mastered the art of cloud dancing.

Just before he left the boy for good, the old man sat with him on the rock. They had already caught their limit, and the noon sun warmed them as the gentle spray of the rapids below them formed a rainbow that skirted half of the rock. This place, the old man reminisced, reminded him of the spot he had fished as a boy on the Pearl River. There, he had learned something about the river which he now taught the boy. "Listen," he said simply. The boy heard the electric rush of the rapids near them, full of energy and vigor, and then, a little farther downstream, the stronger, steadier, and quieter current of the river as it matured. Farther still, the boy heard the river slow down, content with where it was going, still steady but taking its time. "The river," the old man explained, "is a child, an adult, an old woman…all at once. We are like that." He trailed off and stared downstream before continuing. "Yes, the river is young and old at the same time—always moving one into the other: fish eat, lay their eggs, get eaten by the heron, which lays its eggs, and so on. The river itself shifts its course season to season, even week to week. Spring floods, storms, a fallen tree. But this rock that we sit and dance on does not move. This is the place to be…if you are brave enough to wade out this far. Come here when you are troubled. Or, better yet, take this place with you in your heart. Then you can sit and dance here anywhere you are. Think of this place when you build your own bamboo rod."

That was the last time the boy saw him. They had built only the one fly rod together, but the boy had never attempted one on his own. Now, with the disturbing sounds of his parents' argument upstairs intensifying, he was ready again to visit in his mind the saddle-shaped rock midstream. Like a marksman, he lifted the rod blanks one at a time up onto his shoulder and stared with one eye down the shafts: they were straight and smooth. He could sense the tight-knit fiber within, and he shook the blanks in a mock cast to test their strength and flexibility. He was impressed. The stems had already been cut and split into thin strips, which were then planed and glued together by hand. He felt for the thickest and strongest of the strips— along this strip he measured and marked the places to fasten the guides. If the guides weren't placed just right along this strip, the rod would be weak and would arc to one side during the cast. While he was measuring, the sounds of his parents fighting gradually faded and soon all was silent upstairs.

With a dab of epoxy, he cemented the rod tip in place and then scored the base with rough sandpaper to make it take the glue better. Next, he used a tapered reamer to bore out the hole in the cork handle, slid it snugly over the base of the rod blank, and glued it into place. He drank bottled water and ate smoked fish and dried fruit that had been stored in the cellar ages ago and never seemed to run out. It felt like days and weeks were drifting past, like bubbles forming and bursting time and again on the river.

He pressed the first guide firmly up against the blank and wound the silk thread around each post. This had to be done carefully so that the wraps would be symmetrical, balanced, and secure. He ran a small length of thread along the post and then started winding the thread back over itself and around the blank. He then rolled the blank slowly between his fingers, wrapping each coil of thread so that it was tight and snug up against its neighbor. With each turn of the winding silk, time passed, so that when he had nearly finished with the first guide, his classmates had graduated high school.

Next, he layed a separate section of thread in a loop over the winding area and up beyond it, past where the wrap would finish. Patiently, he continued winding until he reached the loop. He cut the winding thread then and ran it through the loop. Carefully, he pulled the loop down back through the winding, the cut end with it, so that the end of the line emerged midway through the wrapped line. With a razor, he trimmed the excess and used a thread burnisher to push the coils closely together. He worked from the outside in to close any gaps. By the time he had finished fastening two guides, three presidents had come and gone. The boy worked on.

After securing four more guides and the hook saver to the rod blanks, he paused, and his classmates, who had long since grown up, launched careers, and started families, by now had grown old and died. And when he reached the point of binding the ferrules to cap the ends of both sections of the fly rod, several generations had passed. Still, the boy worked, unpreturbed.

He brushed on a thin layer of varnish over the wrapped line, for strength and protection against the elements. With the exacto knife, he etched his name directly into the base, just above the cork handle, before giving the entire rod a final coat of varnish. His work was slow and meticulous. In the end, the bamboo rod was smooth and polished—the best he could do and a work of art. In the time it had taken him to create it, the world had seen great technological advances, discoveries in science and medicine, numerous stories of courage and the triumph of the human will. It had survived two major wars, several natural disasters, and one pandemic. None of it reached him.

When he emerged from the cellar, he sensed an enormous chasm between the afternoon he had first opened the brown package and this moment, finally feeling the warm sun again. It felt like ages since he had raised his face up to it, eyes closed, grinning. To the finished rod he attached a fly reel loaded with double-tapered line, took out the small box of Blue-Winged Olives the old man had given him once, and walked in the direction of the river, through the woods, and down to his favorite spot. Wading carefully out to the saddle-shaped rock midstream, he climbed up and prepared to cast. He felt the beautiful bamboo rod, solid in his casting hand. It was light and perfectly balanced—an extension of his arm. What else could he do but go fishing?

As he raised his rod, images streamed into his mind—the pretty girl with the thick glasses, his parents (he *did* miss them), even the bully with the tongue stud—they all rushed up around him. In the sounds of the rapids, he heard the voices of loved ones he had known, and those he might have known. He heard the cries of a baby, the shouts of playing children, the moans of lovemaking, wedding vows, the greetings of old friends, arguments, applause, weeping, the quiet laughter of old people. These were the currents that drove the river, and he had missed his chance to enter it. His heart ached. It was too late now. Or was it? Now that his work on the rod was finally finished, he felt he could begin. He knew that he was ready to come down from the rock, and that soon, very soon, he would. He was ready to fall in love, to do battle, to enjoy children and family, to begin new works of art. He knew he was ready.

With the rod arcing splendidly back and forth between ten and two o'clock, he swung the line in ever expanding spirals. His line traced the shape of a sideways figure eight, the symbol of infinity. And as he swayed to the rhythm of his casting, he began to dance.

ABOUT THE AUTHOR

Mathew V. Spano has published poetry, short stories, and essays over the last twenty years. His work has appeared in various publications, such as *The Los Angeles Times*, *Psychological Perspectives*, *Quantum Fairy Tales*, *The Yellow Chair Review*, *Frogpond*, *Cicada*, *This Broken Shore*, *The Heron's Nest*, and *Middlesex*, as well as in anthologies, such as *Palisades, Parkways & Pinelands (Blast Press, 2016)*; *Baseball Haiku: The Best Haiku Ever Written About the Game (W.W. Norton & Co., 2007)*; and *The Poets of New Jersey: From Colonial to Contemporary (Jersey Shore Publications, 2005)*. He has been teaching English Composition and Mythology in Literature as a full-time professor for over twenty years at Middlesex County College in Edison, NJ where he also serves as Freshman Composition Coordinator and Co-Director of the MCC Honors Program. He earned his Ph.D. in Comparative Literature from Rutgers University in New Brunswick, NJ, his dissertation focusing on the works of pioneering psychologist Carl Jung and Nobel laureate Hermann Hesse. Mat is also the founder and owner of the online store *haiku 4u* (www.zazzle.com/haiku4u) featuring merchandise with his poetry and artwork. He lives with his wife Stephanie and their two children in central NJ where the family enjoys fishing, hiking, and searching for critters under rocks—especially along Ken Lockwood Gorge.

WHYS & WHEREFORES

Meet Me in Botswana:
What Is Blast Press?

A speech for national poetry month about BLAST PRESS.

Ab li dolen in l'air [look up: beauty falls from the air] "A book should be a ball of light in your hands." ~~Ezra Pound

As we all know, April is "International Guitar Month." But my heart twangs for poetry, and I was invited here to tell you a little bit about a tiny poetry publishing company called **BLAST PRESS**.

Description of BLAST PRESS

BLAST PRESS is what I would call a "micro-publisher." We usually publish chapbooks—booklets under 100 pages in length. Our print runs are usually under 100 copies per edition. And **BLAST PRESS** has published over 100 chapbooks from some 20 authors in its career. The entire cost is assumed by **BLAST PRESS**, so we are the publisher, and not a vanity press or service.

BLAST PRESS has been sustaining its small operation—in the black, mind you, no small feat—for about 20 years now. We have had a few more ambitious titles where the book itself, the author, and **BLAST**

PRESS decide to dedicate the extra resources needed to make the event a success.

Part of the **BLAST PRESS** ethos is to keep the authors in charge of their work so that they can maintain maximum control of their creative material in the out-lying years and don't need to be writing to **BLAST PRESS** for permission to re-publish snippets or poems.

BLAST PRESS
324B Matawan Avenue
Cliffwood, NJ 07721
(732) 970-8409
gregglory.com

Our Credo
Do not dispraise the light
That, singing whatever's brightest,
Undoes the theft of night—
—Touch to caress, or move to love,
As this thoughtless rhyme does prove.

From **Ascent**

A Solitary Headstone

Niggling addendum to "Meet me in Botswana"

Magazines, published with a week's, month's, quarter's or even a year's date grow elderly on the shelves in a way that a collection of one individual's work never can. What year does Shakespeare's book expire? Horace is renewed year by year, no matter how worn his saws may wane. But a magazine or casual collection of miscellaneous artifacts, no matter how august the individual members of the find, retain an interest for us mostly as a time capsule. Even the Egyptian tombs of the pharaohs hold more interest for us because of what they reveal about the era of their creation than for what they say about their putative occupants. Old poetry quarterlies are no different, although they may contain an Endymion.

This is why **BLAST PRESS** is dedicated to publishing single-author volumes and stand-alone essay collections almost exclusively. Unless a poet is unknown, there is no point in his publication being undertaken by a small press. And if an author is unknown, he is best presented to an unacquainted public in his own exclusive company. It is always wisest to let a guest unroll at least a few of his favorite tales before we escort him from the house. What is characteristic and worthwhile in the poet's voice will quietly assert itself over the course of his varied pieces much better than if we merely heard his alba or evensong in isolation, let alone in the cacophonous squawk of a miscellany. To the marriage of true minds, ours and the author's, let not serial publication admit impediments.

Only appearing in magazines and periodicals is like never having a final resting place—a poet without a plot.

ALSO AVAILABLE

123

The Giant in the Cradle
Gregg Glory
[Gregg G. Brown]

List Price: $4.50
5.06" x 7.81"
Black & White on Cream
136 pages
ISBN-13: 978-1492396055
ISBN-10:1492396052
BISAC: Poetry / American

FROM THE POEM "HEIGHT OF SUMMER"

Here is the day, the bridal day undaunted;
Here noon, at highest noon... hesitates...
The height of summer, at its crest arrested,
Held between warm hands to kiss—
The levitated real at pause in sun's perfection;
Paused because we cannot see, cannot imagine
Beyond such ripeness—

Yoga Notes
Carrie Pedersen Hudak

List Price: $4.50
5" x 8"
66 pages
ISBN-13: 978-1494330958
ISBN-10: 1494330954
BISAC: Body, Mind &
Spirit

From the first essay: Just Practice

When I tell people I am a yoga teacher, they often say, I
could never do yoga. I can't even touch my toes. Great, I
say, you are already practicing awareness, that's part of
the practice. Can you breathe? If you can breathe, then
you can do yoga.

West of Home
Joe Weil, Emily Vogel

List Price: $10.00
Paperback: 98 pages
ISBN-10: 0615878415
ISBN-13:9780615878416
8 x 5 inches

From the Introduction

"West of Home" is a collaborative book of poetry which reflects the present and ongoing sentiments of Joe Weil and Emily Vogel. It includes 14 "responsorial" poems (call and response), between the two poets, as they respond to one another's themes and ideas, as well as two sections of poems, one for each poet's individual work.

Self-Symponies
Daniel   Weeks

List Price: $10.00
Paperback: 146 pages
ISBN-10: 0692238581
ISBN-13:978-0692238585
7.4 x 9.7 inches

From the Introduction

Inspired by listening to the four symphonies of Johannes
Brahms, Daniel Weeks's Self-Symphonies explore the
landscapes, cityscapes, and seascapes that are the
backdrop to a life lived on the New Jersey shore. The
four long poems in this collection provide meditations
on family, inheritance, and loss, society, nature, and
culture, and stasis and change--all of the elements that
Coleridge said bething the individual self.

The Pilot Light
Gregg Glory
[Gregg G. Brown]

List Price: $5.50
Paperback: 132 pages
ISBN-13: 9781511941921
5.5 x 8.5 inches

About *The Pilot Light*

The poems in Gregg Glory's The Pilot Light are about relationships—with family, friends, and lovers—along with reminiscences of a childhood spent close to nature in the New Jersey countryside. Glory is particularly adept at exploring the significant and oftentimes intimate moments that define our most important relationships, moments which, in turn, help us create the story of the self.

Knowing the Moment
Emanuel di Pasquale

List Price: $12.95
Paperback: 131 pages
ISBN-13: 9781503117471
5.5 x 8.5 inches

About *Knowing the Moment*

Emanuel di Pasquale has never been one to shy away from the more difficult aspects of living a full and engaged human life, and Knowing the Moment is perhaps his most searing work in this regard, as he confronts the hardships he encountered while growing up in his native Sicily. But these kinds of revelations are never the final word in his poetry. Tough times always seem to point him back to love—as he casts his mind back to life in Sicily or engages with the present in his poems about Long Branch, N.J.

The   Hummingbird's Apprentice
  Gregg Glory
  [Gregg G. Brown]

List Price: $4.50
Paperback: 159 pages
ISBN-10: 1511941928
ISBN-13: 9781511941921
5.1 x 7.8 inches

From *The Hummingbird's Apprentice*

ROADSIDE WINE

Pull off 71 suddenly, onto
a wide shoulder of dust and grass.
weigh down a length
of brown barbwire fence
like a wave of honey breaking.
Excited, splash ankle-deep
into the unhurrying surf
full of velvety bee sounds, and select
one perfect blossom. It is
so sweet in the slow afternoon.
And, where you've cut your thumb,
a thrill of air catches.

American Songbook
Gregg Glory
[Gregg G. Brown]

List Price: $3.75
Paperback: 98 pages
ISBN-10: 1482703297
ISBN-13: 9780692238585
5.5 x 8.5 inches

The Old Truculence

A note concerning the basic arc of this book of poems—to re-register grace and freedom as America's primary metier.

Freedom breeds elegance. Not the inbred elegance of aristocracy, where beautiful ladies eventually come to resemble their Russian wolfhounds. Nor, simply, the truculent elegance of that sly Benjamin Franklin who, as ambassador to the French Court, refused to bow before King Louis the 16th or doff his coonskin cap.

Freedom breeds the desire to create one meaningful action with your entire life—the effortful elegance of the artist that James Joyce defined as the willingness to gamble your whole life on the wrong idea, a bad aesthetic, or, it may be, a genuine triumph. And America has created, and can still create, a unique scale of opportunity for such elegant "throws of the dice," as Mallarme might say. A natty Fred Astaire (originally Austerlitz), gliding with the ease of an ice skater as he

backs Rita Hayworth (a gal from Brooklyn) into
immortality to a tune penned by the jewish Jerome Kern
in an industry patented in the U.S.A. is but one example
of the scale of that opportunity.

When you are free to do anything, a desire grows in
the breast not to do just anything, but to do the best
thing—and that is an aesthetic dilemma. The mere
accumulation of capital, or the arbitrary exercise by
minor government regulators of petty power, are two
classic examples of the desire for a meaningful
expression of life-status that lack the aesthetic instinct.
Such timid ambitions grow most strongly where the full
range of light is narrowed, and the blossom of selfhood
must twist around corners to open its ruby glory in a
thinning patch of sunlight.

Gregg Glory
March, 2013

Come, My Dreams
Come gather round me, multitudinous dreams
That in the dim twilight are murmuring soft;
Come lay by my head in the pillow-seam;
Come carry my freighted heart aloft.

O, I would dare dream as few men dream
Beyond the cruel cudgel of the strong,
Beyond the purpled tapestries of is and seems
Hung before my eyes, beyond cold right or wrong.

Made in the USA
Charleston, SC
16 August 2016